Marriage Means Love

MARRIAGE MEANS LOVE

A Celebration of Togetherness

Selected by Shifra Stein

Illustrated by Lilian Weytjens

♕ Hallmark Crown Editions

Marriage is many worlds…
…it's a fountain overflowing
with the fullness of life,
…a garden of discovery
and rich delight,
…a haven where
two lovers unite.

...a fountain overflowing
with the fullness of life...

The more you love, the more love you are given to love with.

Lucien Price

A GOOD
MARRIAGE

A good marriage—which means a continually improving
marriage—is a spiritual experience... Its joys are in the constant,
loving effort to understand and help each other. Its happiness is
in learning to share, in the lifelong transformation of "alone"
into "together."

Virginia and Louis Baldwin

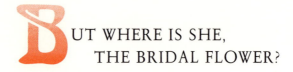

BUT WHERE IS SHE, THE BRIDAL FLOWER?

from *In Memoriam*

But where is she, the bridal flower
That must be made a wife ere noon?
She enters, glowing like the moon
Of Eden on its bridal bower:

On me she bends her blissful eyes
And then on thee; they meet thy look
And brighten like the star that shook
Betwixt the palms of paradise.

O when her life was yet in bud,
He too foretold the perfect rose.
For thee she grew, for thee she grows
For ever, and as fair as good.

And thou art worthy; full of power;
As gentle; liberal-minded, great,
Consistent; wearing all that weight
Of learning lightly like a flower.

But now set out; the noon is near,
And I must give away the bride;
She fears not, or with thee beside
And me behind her, will not fear.

6

Now sign your names, which shall be read,
Mute symbols of a joyful morn,
By village eyes as yet unborn;
The names are sign'd, and overhead

Begins the clash and clang that tells
The joy to every wandering breeze;
The blind wall rocks, and on the trees
The dead leaf trembles to the bells.

O happy hour, and happier hours
Await them. Many a merry face
Salutes them—maidens of the place,
That pelt us to the porch with flowers.

Alfred, Lord Tennyson

7

MARRIED LOVE

Married living needs the continuance of the dash and sparkle of romantic love. But the relation of romantic love to married love is somewhat like that of a little tree to the larger tree which it later becomes. It has life and fresh young energy that enables it to grow. When it has grown into a larger tree, its heart and vitality are still there, but, with continued life, it has taken new rings of growth, its branches have spread wider and its roots have gone deeper. Moreover, it bears flowers and fruit which the little tree did not produce.

Married love is love woven into a pattern of living. It has in it the elements of understanding and of the passionate kindness of husband and wife toward each other. It is rich in the many-sided joys of life because each is more concerned with giving joy than with grasping it for himself. And joys are most truly experienced when they are most fully shared.

Leland Foster Wood

LIVING TOGETHER

As you live together, you will discover, accept and, hopefully, enjoy each other as real people. Your flexibility is your strength. You are not set in your ways, rigid and uncompromising. You are willing to be shown, to discover one another. Marriage will test your adaptability. You are products of completely different family upbringing. You have your own tastes, your own standards, your expectations of what marriage will bring.

Mary Anne Guitar

There are explanations of love
in all languages
and not one found wiser than this:

There is a place where love begins
and a place where love ends—
and love asks nothing.

Carl Sandburg

It's hard to give myself and have the gift returned...but at least I don't have the old feeling, the old emptiness because of all I may have missed from playing safe.

Dean Walley

Those who have never known the deep intimacy and the intense companionship of happy mutual love have missed the best thing that life has to give....

Bertrand Russell

OVE'S PHILOSOPHY

The fountains mingle with the river
And the rivers with the ocean,
The winds of heaven mix forever
With a sweet emotion;
Nothing in the world is single,
All things by a law divine
In one another's being mingle—
Why not I with thine?

See the mountains kiss high heaven,
And the waves clasp one another;
No sister-flower would be forgiven
If it disdain'd its brother;
And the sunlight clasps the earth,
And the moonbeams kiss the sea—
What are all these kissings worth,
If thou kiss not me?

Percy Bysshe Shelley

THE HONEYMOON PHASE

During the early years of marriage, we are still in the honeymoon phase, still have the sense of spontaneous mutual understanding and complete sameness. By instinct, we choose partners complementary to ourselves. What each one has repressed in himself during the period of adolescent differentiation, he rediscovers in his partner. Hence the wonderful feeling of completeness in each other.

Paul Tournier

The most important single solution to our problems in family life is our potential capacity to care for each other, to love in the truest and broadest sense of that word and to increase that capacity throughout life.

William Menninger, M.D.

We have a great vocabulary for hostility, but we need new ways to say "I love you." Receiving affection throws people into more of a crisis than being yelled at. People need both. It's the sound of two hands clapping.

Betty Dederich

Let there be spaces in your togetherness.

Kahlil Gibran

True love will never come undone.
It is as big as all
Eternity
And higher than the sun.

We must, we must, take time,
    take time, to kiss;
If we do not,
We miss.

Jesse Stuart

It is only important to love
        the world...to regard the world
and ourselves and all beings
        with love, admiration and respect.

Hermann Hesse

# A GOOD MARRIAGE

A good marriage is one where love is not destroyed. Love changes, of course, in its manifestation as time goes on and as individuals achieve higher levels of maturity, but change does not mean destruction. It can and should mean growth. A good marriage is one which allows for change and growth in the individuals and in the way they express their love.

Pearl S. Buck

Living in marriage, if you choose to live it with love and work at it with all your heart, is the best human life there is.

Robert Raynolds

CONTINUITY
THROUGH FREEDOM

Only when one is connected to one's own core is one connected to others.…When you love someone, you do not love them all the time, in exactly the same way, from moment to moment. It is an impossibility. It is even a lie to pretend to. And yet this is exactly what most of us demand. We have so little faith in the ebb and flow of life, of love, of relationships. We leap at the flow of the tide and resist in terror its ebb. We are afraid it will never return. We insist on permanency, on duration, on continuity; when the only continuity possible, in life as in love, is in growth, in fluidity—in freedom, in the sense that the dancers are free, barely touching as they pass, but partners in the same pattern.

…There is no one-and-only; there are just one-and-only moments.

The one-and-only moments are justified. Even a temporary return to them is valid. Finding shells together, polishing chestnuts, sharing one's treasures—all these moments of together-aloneness are valid, but not permanent.

One comes to realize that there is no permanent pure relationship, and there should not be. It is not even something to be desired. The pure relationship is limited, in space and in time. In its essence, it implies exclusion. It excludes the rest of life, other relationships, other sides of personality, other responsibilities, other possibilities in the future. The race on the beach together renews one's youth like a dip in the sea. But we are no longer children; life is not a beach. There is no pattern here for permanent return, only for refreshment....

All living relationships are in process of change, of expansion, and must perpetually be building themselves new forms.

Anne Morrow Lindbergh

Love does not dominate; it cultivates.

Goethe

Love will teach us all things:
    but we must learn how to win love;
it is got with difficulty:
    it is a possession dearly bought
with much labor and in long time;
    for one must love not sometimes only,
        for a passing moment, but always.

Fyodor Dostoevsky
from The Brothers Karamazov

...a garden of discovery
and rich delight...

THE PRECIOUS INGREDIENT

It is good to know that you are loved just as you are. Instinctively you feel grateful to the one who so loves you that he will accept and endure the weaknesses which beset you and which you have not yet learned to overcome. Life is peaceful and pleasant on this basis....

Love is an art. Marriage is an art. The art of love in marriage can be learned. But all the time we must keep in mind that the precious ingredient in our marriage is love.

Dr. David Goodman

HOW TO SAY YOU LOVE HIM

Go for a walk in the new-fallen snow together at dusk.

Pick up a romantic collection of medieval poetry for his nightstand.

Give his car a secret name that only you two can comprehend.

Discuss emotions. Yours about him.

Call his mother…

Write his name in the snow, if there is any. Or write it on the icebox.

Put your picture in a paperweight for him.

Put two "I Love You" notes in his socks.

Pick him a four-leaf clover.

Send him a "Wish You Were Here" postcard from your house.

Send him a note that says you'd rather fight than switch lovers.

Bite him.

Jani Gardner

What is this need
To touch your face?
As if I were blind,
I reach to touch your face;
You move, just out of reach.

If we had never been lovers,
Would you mind so much?
If we had never been lovers,
Would I need to?

Ione Hill

Yesterday on the street,
I saw someone from the back
and thought he was you.
I ran to him,
calling your name....
And when he turned,
seeing my surprise
and disappointment,
he looked disappointed, too,
knowing he wasn't the one...
knowing his wasn't the face
that brings me such joy.

Julia Summers

26

in love
we are drawn in a long curve
like the rising of light
across the photographed globe

in love
we taste other mouths
indifferent

original
in every earthly touch
in love we repeat motions
we repeat love
we repeat our rising of love
like the fierce scanning of light
across the moving earth

Joyce Carol Oates

MARRIAGE'S BRIGHT BEGINNINGS

I scent the air…
Of blessings, when I come
　　but near the house.
What a delicious breath
Marriage sends forth—
The violet bed's not sweeter.

Thomas Middleton

Plant a flower in a pot and its growth is limited to the size of the container; in fact, the container may stunt the growth of the flower. But plant it in a field and something different happens. Open to the sunlight and air, with space to expand, it can grow to the extent of its inherent capacity for growth....Marriage should be a positive affirmation of our desire to grow and expand our love and identity through, with, and to others.

Nena and George O'Neill

7 A.M.

The first time you saw
my early morning face,
rumpled, wrinkled, whiskered,
I thought the whole thing was over...
but then you kissed me,
soft as sun through fog,
and I knew that the whole thing
had just begun.

Kenneth Holt

MARRIED LOVE: AN ART

Married love is an art, a great art, worthy for its rewards of our highest efforts. It contains practical elements:

1. Generosity as well as good sense in money matters.
2. Understanding of each other's sexual personality, so that each may give pleasure as well as receive it.
3. Cooperation in the training of the children.
4. Unity in religious belief, parents and children going to church as one family.
5. Acceptance of in-laws in cordial hospitality.

Dr. David Goodman

31

Marriage begins
       with the first look
  …and the first kiss.
The first look
     between lover and beloved
divides the intoxication of Life…
    …from the awakening.

Kahlil Gibran

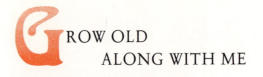

GROW OLD ALONG WITH ME

Grow old along with me!
The best is yet to be,
The last of life, for which
   the first was made:
Our times are in his hand
Who saith, "A whole I planned,
Youth shows but half;
   trust God: see all, nor be afraid!"

Robert Browning
from *Rabbi Ben Ezra*

OPAL

You are ice and fire,
The touch of you burns my hands like snow.
You are cold and flame.
You are the crimson of amaryllis,
The silver of moon-touched magnolias.
When I am with you,
My heart is a frozen pond
Gleaming with agitated torches.

Amy Lowell

Loving
Is a good way
To stay
Married.

Marie Costan

Love is playful, noble and ennobled,
O shattering gentleness!
the sober, sweet glee
of its flowing wonder!

Kenneth Patchen

35

Love is a symbol of eternity.
It wipes out all sense of time,
destroying all memory of a beginning
and all fear of an end.

Anne Louise de Stael

Love is eternal.
The aspect may change,
but not the essence.

Vincent van Gogh

There may be more beautiful times: but this one is ours.

Jean-Paul Sartre

Blessed is the marriage which
in the tumult of the world
has the quiet of love.

Katherine Nelson Davis

38

THE COUPLE IN THE PHOTO

They seem so unposed,
    so easy in their love.
        Note:
    his protective arm,
    her contented smile.
It's as though they couldn't imagine
    being anywhere
        but together.
    Beautiful, don't you think,
    that after all this time
    those two happy people
      are still
      us.

Ed Cunningham

...a haven where
two lovers unite...

Song

You bound strong sandals on my feet,
　　You gave me bread and wine,
And sent me under sun and stars,
　　For all the world was mine.

Oh, take the sandals off my feet,
　　You know not what you do;
For all my world is in your arms,
　　My sun and stars are you.

Sara Teasdale

41

MARRIAGE SONG

Judah Halevi, an outstanding poet
of the Middle Ages whose hymns
are embodied in the Jewish prayer book,
wrote many love songs.

Fair is my dove, my loved one,
    None can with her compare:
Yea, comely as Jerusalem,
    Like unto Tirzah fair.

Shall she in tents unstable
    A wanderer abide,
While in my heart awaits her
    A dwelling deep and wide?

The magic of her beauty
    Has stolen my heart away:
Not Egypt's wise enchanters
    Held half such wondrous sway.

E'en as the changing opal
    In varying lustre glows,
Her face at every moment
    New charms and sweetness shows.

White lilies and red roses
    There blossom on one stem:
Her lips of crimson berries
    Tempt mine to gather them.

By dusky tresses shaded
    Her brow gleams fair and pale,
Like to the sun at twilight,
    Behind a cloudy veil.

Her beauty shames the day-star,
    And makes the darkness light:
Day in her radiant presence
    Grows seven times more bright.

This is a lonely lover!
    Come, fair one, to his side,
That happy be together
    The bridegroom and the bride!

Judah Halevi

# MY BRIDE

She is devout, my bride.
Who more devout than she?
More devout than my bride
Only an angel can be.

She is lovely, my bride.
Who more lovely than she?
Lovelier than my bride
Only the sun can be.

She is good, my bride.
Who better than she?
Better than my bride
Nobody can be.

Joseph Rolnik

You are
All there is,
Has been
      and
Will be.
So
What you are,
Have become
      and
Shall be
    is
Through your love
What I am.

Gordon Parks

SPECTRUM

Color of dusk, this room at five o'clock,
Color of waiting....Suddenly the rhythm
Falters, begins to quicken as the lock
Turns and he enters, fills the room, brings with him
Color of my contentment. The hour, surmounted,
Completes itself—color of blessings, counted.

Maureen Cannon

TO MY DEAR
AND LOVING HUSBAND

If ever two were one, then surely we.
If ever man were lov'd by wife, then thee.
If ever wife was happy in a man,
Compare with me, ye women, if you can.
I prize thy love more than whole mines of gold,
Or all the riches that the East doth hold.
My love is such that rivers cannot quench,
Nor ought but love from thee give recompense.
Thy love is such I can no way repay;
The heavens reward thee manifold I pray.
Then while we live, in love let's so persevere,
That when we live no more, we may live ever.

Anne Bradstreet

"THE OTHER"

Marriage is not at all what romantic lovers imagine it to be; it is an institution founded upon an instinct; to be successful, it requires not only physical attraction, but willpower, patience, and the always difficult acceptance of "the other"; finally, if these conditions are fulfilled, a beautiful and lasting affection can be established—a unique and, to those who have never known it, incomprehensible mingling of love, friendship, sensuality, and respect....

André Maurois

LET ME NOT
TO THE MARRIAGE OF TRUE MINDS

Sonnet CXVI

Let me not to the marriage of true minds
Admit impediments. Love is not love
Which alters when it alteration finds,
Or bends with the remover to remove:
O, no! it is an ever-fixed mark
That looks on tempests and is never shaken;
It is the star to every wand'ring bark,
Whose worth's unknown, although his
    height be taken.
Love's not Time's fool, though rosy lips
    and cheeks
Within his bending sickle's compass come;
Love alters not with his brief hours and weeks,
But bears it out even to the edge of doom: —
If this be error and upon me proved,
I never writ, nor no man ever loved.

William Shakespeare

LOVE LETTER

In a classic message of love to his Johanna,
Otto von Bismarck, the German chancellor, speaks his heart:

…We ought to share with each other joy and suffering—I your suffering and you mine; that we are not united for the sake of showing and sharing with each other only that which gives pleasure; but that you may pour out your heart at all times to me and I to you, whatever it may contain; that I must and will bear your sorrows, your thoughts, your naughtinesses, if you have any, and love you as you are—not as you ought to be or might be. Make me serviceable, use me for what purpose you will, ill-treat me without and within, if you have the wish to do so. I am there for that purpose, at your disposal; but never be embarrassed in any way with me. Trust me unreservedly, in the conviction that I accept everything that comes from you with profound love, whether it be glad or patient. Do not keep your gloomy thoughts for yourself while you look on me with cheerful brow and merry eyes, but share with me in word and look what you have in your heart, whether it be blessing or sorrow.

Oh, what a love it was, utterly free, unique, like nothing else on earth! Their thoughts were like other people's songs.... They loved each other because everything around them willed it, the trees and the clouds and the sky over their heads and the earth under their feet....

Never, never, even in their moments of richest and wildest happiness, were they unaware of a sublime joy in the total design of the universe, a feeling that they themselves were a part of that whole, an element in the beauty of the cosmos.

Boris Pasternak
from Doctor Zhivago

from THE SONG OF SONGS

Chapter II

Hark! my beloved! behold, he cometh,
Leaping upon the mountains, skipping upon the hills.
My beloved is like a gazelle or a young hart;
Behold, he standeth behind our wall,
He looketh in through the windows,
He peereth through the lattice.
My beloved spoke, and said unto me:
"Rise up, my love, my fair one, and come away.
For, lo, the winter is past,
The rain is over and gone;
The flowers appear on the earth;
The time of singing is come,
And the voice of the turtledove is heard in our land...."

Solomon

And if I ever think love is futile,
   I'll think of you and know
   that love is all that matters.
Futility is only a guess, a despair,
   but love is everything
   and worth all the risks.

Naomi Sheldon

LOVE POEMS
OF ANCIENT EGYPT

Knowing for certain that you love me
I nestle at your side.

My heart is sure that among all
Men you are the main one for me.

The whole world shines
I wish we could go on sleeping together,
Like this, to the end of eternity.

Tranquil our paths
When your hand rests on mine in joy.

Your voice gives life, like nectar.

To see you is more than food or drink.

MAN AND WOMAN

Then the Lord God said,
    "It is not good that the man is alone;
I will make him a helper
    like himself."
The Lord God cast the man
    into a deep sleep and, while he slept,
took one of his ribs and closed up
    its place with flesh.
And the rib which the Lord God
    took from the man, he made into a woman,
and brought her to him.
    Then the man said, "She now is
bone of my bone, and flesh of my flesh;
    she shall be called Woman,
for from man she has been taken."
    For this reason a man leaves his father
and mother, and clings to his wife,
    and the two become one flesh.

Genesis 2:18, 21-24

But if you love
and must needs have desires,
let these be your desires:
To melt and be like a running brook
that sings its melody to the night.
To know the pain
of too much tenderness.
To be wounded
by your own understanding of love;
And to bleed willingly and joyfully.

Kahlil Gibran

THE SOLITAIRE

Summer and winter, day and night,
dreams come true by the clear white light
of this treasured symbol, this fiery splinter
from love's own heart.

Through summer or winter
the setting's a forecast, a golden rumor
of blessings to come.

And winter or summer
precious memories of courtship stay
locked in its beauty, night or day.

Florence Jacobs

from **D**OVER BEACH

Ah, love, let us be true
To one another for the world, which
     seems
To lie before us like a land of dreams,
So various, so beautiful, so new,
Hath really neither joy, nor love, nor
     light,
Nor certitude, nor peace, nor help for
     pain;
And we are here as on a darkling plain
Swept with confused alarms of struggle
     and flight,
Where ignorant armies clash by night.

Matthew Arnold

MIDCENTURY LOVE LETTER

Stay near me. Speak my name. Oh, do not wander
By a thought's span, heart's impulse, from the light
We kindle here. You are my sole defender
(As I am yours) in this precipitous night,
Which over earth, till common landmarks alter,
Is falling, without stars, and bitter cold.
We two have but our burning selves for shelter.
Huddle against me. Give me your hand to hold.

So might two climbers lost in mountain weather
On a high slope and taken by the storm,
Desperate in the darkness, cling together
Under one cloak and breathe each other warm.
Stay near me. Spirit, perishable as bone,
In no such winter can survive alone.

Phyllis McGinley

WEDDING SONG

(There Is Love)

He is now to be among you
At the calling of your hearts
Rest assured, this troubador is acting on his part
The union of your spirits here has caused him to
    remain
For whenever two or more of you are gathered in
    his name
There is love, there is love.

Well a man shall leave his mother and a woman leave
    her home
They shall travel on to where the two shall be
    as one
As it was in the beginning, is now, and till the end
Woman draws her life from man and gives it back
    again
And there is love, there is love.

Well then what's to be the reason for becoming man
    and wife?
Is it love that brings you here or love that brings
    you life?
For if loving is the answer
Then who's the giving for?

Do you believe in something that you've never
    seen before?
Oh, there's love, oh, there's love.

Oh, the marriage of your spirits here
Has caused him to remain
For whenever two or more of you
Are gathered in his name
There is love, there is love.

Noel Stookey

Marriage is a fusion of two hearts—the union of two lives—the coming together of two tributaries which, after being joined in marriage, will flow in the same channel in the same direction…carrying the same burdens of responsibility and obligation.

Peter Marshall

Love is a journey
The moment it begins
The journey's all it is
No matter where it ends.
Mason Williams

I LOVE TO HAVE YOU TOUCH ME

"I love to have you touch me."
…has to be among
the warmest things
    a woman can
say to a man.

Dick Sutphen

You walk into a forever world…
walk with love.

Indian Wedding Song

WANT AD

One human being
To share my life
For as long as possible.
Opportunity for love,
Unlimited.

Shifra Stein

I love you
I desire you
and oh
I long to soothe you
to calm you
to caress you
and then
to gently smooth you
trust me
I mean it
you know
you've seen it
my soul, my spirit
you've come so near it
take it don't fear it

there's so much to gain
this sorrow and pain
is only the rain
washing clear what remains
of slow-to-go stains
but love overcomes
when two become one
I'll bear half your burdens
I'll bear you a son
we've born such fine happiness
that can't be undone
trust me
I mean it
you know
you've seen it.   Mary Lee

Printed on Hallmark Crown Royale Book paper. Set in Romanee,
a twentieth-century typeface designed by Jan van Krimpen of Holland.
Romanee was created to accompany the only surviving italic
of the seventeenth-century typefounder Christoffel Van Dijck.
Designed by Lilian Weytjens.